Att...
Training
Releasing Youth

Adrian Hawkes

New Wine Press

New Wine Press
P.O. Box 17
Chichester
England PO20 6YB

ISBN 0 947852 89 1

By the same author:
Leadership and . . .

Contents

Thanks

For help in the preparation of this book to Anita Brookes and Shyamala Thambiah, longsuffering secretaries who constantly try to sort me out.

To my wife, Pauline, for always encouraging me to be and do more, and pushing me on when I flag.

To the Church of Pentecost in Accra, Ghana, for it was while there that I managed to bring much of the main part of the hard work of writing a book to a conclusion.

And to Dave Tomlinson, who, although I'm sure he doesn't know it, was the inspiration for me to write the book. That doesn't of course mean he will agree with it all! And to Julia Twinam for her pictures which make the printed word more memorable.

Here it is. My prayer is that it will help those who want to get hold of young people, keep them in God, and release them to do the work of the Kingdom.

About the Author

by Jeff Lucas

Adrian Hawkes is a man who was used by God in his youth, and since that time has consistently demonstrated a heart to see young people flourish in the Kingdom.

As a teenager, Adrian was the leader of a group that rejoiced in the name "The Ribbons of Faith", a group which majored on village evangelism, and later spearheaded outreach efforts to rockers in the Birmingham "Bullring" area. Obviously Adrian scorned the idea that God could only use "older" or "qualified" people. It was a good thing he did, as his efforts drew crowds of up to 400.

During his time at Bible College Adrian became the leader of a group of young students who pioneered a church planted in Dorking.

Five years were spent building up the previously small work in Grangetown, near Middlesborough, and then the Hawkes family moved to London to take on two churches with a combined membership of less than fifty. Since that time the churches have seen considerable growth, with several hundred currently in attendance, satellite churches planted and a large staff employed.

But figures and statistics, while impressive, don't really tell the whole story. The truth behind the figures is that Adrian has consistently believed that "church" is far more than a narrow band of activity centering around a religious building on one or two days a week. Rather his philosophy has been far broader, believing that life in the Kingdom of God is about touching every facet of life with the life of God. Young people have been the beneficiaries of this broad vision, with day nurseries, schools, colleges, youth opportunity employment programmes and the like being established.

A quick look around the leadership in New Living Ministries will tell a similar story of young people effectively reached, as so many of the leadership team are barely out of their teens!

Of course the true proof of ministry is to be found in the home. Suffice it to say that the Hawkes offspring, Anna (now married to Robert), Carla and Gareth-Illya all love the Lord and in their various ways express that love in the strong working commitment. This is a family that is truly together in the work of God.

As a personal footnote, I would only add that my 7 year old, Richard, deeply believes, and I quote, "that God and Uncle Adrian know everything!" . . . what more can be said?!

Foreword

by Ishmael

The average Pastor needs very little time to define his role and aims. He will be well-pleased if his church has managed to maintain its membership numbers and if the bank balance stays healthy.

Adrian Hawkes and the average Pastor are as opposite as the North and South Poles!

Whilst many men of God could only cope with one annual conceivable project, Adrian only seems to have interest in pursuing things that most people would laugh at as being impossible or way beyond their financial resources.

I suppose that is why Adrian is now not only surrounded by thriving packed assemblies, but has also started his own schools, a college, and has bought a multi-million pound building that is famous for being one of the largest secular rock music venues in London.

This may leave you with a picture of him perched behind a leather topped desk surrounded by telephones and people running to obey his every command.

Nothing could be further from the truth. Adrian is a loving, humble, caring man, a people's person. He has no interest in building his own empire; his only desire is to create brand new ways and means which seem to be beyond people's wildest imaginations, to serve the saints, and to reach the millions of lost and needy around him in the heart of London. You may say I am biased as Adrian is my friend. Well, that may be true, but don't just take my word for it, see for yourself how God has used this man in mind-blowing missions.

I recommend this book to you. You may agree or disagree with what he writes, and that is of course your prerogative. All I ask is that as you read you will hear his heart, then hopefully you will find your own personal vision expanding. Remember, one of the few things that God finds impossible is trying to work with people with little vision and who cannot believe that He can easily make the humanly impossible – possible!

Comments on this Book

by The Author

Youth is a subject that, as a preacher, I have never really had the opportunity or the circumstances to expand on, although I wish I had. In the age-old and ongoing discussion I feel that, even though I do not have all the answers to the problems, I do have some answers that are tried and tested.

There have been forums where I have raised the subject and put forward some of my views, and I often got the impression that people's responses were either:

1. "You are obviously some sort of nut" (me that is).
2. "Your answers never could and never would work for me" (I am mystified as to why they reach this conclusion).

OR

3. "Your answers are not the clichés we have been

11

"Hello dear! Just looking at the world from a different viewpoint."

taught, therefore we can't even hear what you are saying properly"!

So if you look at this book you may find that the answers I give are different from what you expected, different from the ones you hoped I would give. Don't at the first glance say what the others have said, don't take that line and drop it there, or throw the ideas away – be daring, try to think in a new way. Stand on the table, the world looks different from a different view point. Try lateral thinking, shelve your clichés and have some success in this important area of life.

The things I have written in this book are not merely the result of theory or study, though I hope there is some of both, but they are primarily the result of experimentation, experience, and I think others would agree with me, some success in this area.

It should be said that I have heard the subject discussed and even preached about, but sad to say, most of what I hear comes from situations of failure, not success, from cliché-ridden ideas, not from track-record proven action!

In the end that's what counts.

Adrian L Hawkes
(North London, November 1989)

Chapter 1

Live Church

What parents want, what leaders want, what the world needs, is stable young people who know where they are going and who will make a great contribution to society.

I cannot see how any of the above can be achieved without real purpose in people's hearts and lives – the centre of their being. Environment does not always change individuals, but individuals will change their environment.

When the life of Jesus Christ is put into an individual, he comes alive. Life is to be lived, to be taken hold of, to use, to make something with, to be creative with, to be fulfilled. Jesus said that He had come, not to take life but to give life, not just an existence but top-quality, supernatural, vibrant, fulfilling life. That's what Christianity is about. So the first pre-requisite to attracting-training-releasing young people is to introduce them to a real, exciting, relationship with Jesus. He will fill them with life.

I'm sure you'll soon fit in and feel like one of us. . . ."

The great tragedy (which so often occurs) is that the local church tries to tone that life down, not too hard, not too soft, not too long, not too short, anaemic, "balanced", and let's be honest, safe and boring.

The life that Jesus gives to young people is not safe and boring, it is risk-taking, lateral-thinking, creative, world-changing. If you then try to expose that dynamic life to what is often a "boring church", it will create frustration, disillusionment and loss.

However, God is not boring, never has been and never will be. We should not reduce church life to that which is less than God. Being with the church should be the most exciting thing in town. It should be the gathering of the most alive people in your village or city. Christian people are the alive people, through which life should be demonstrated when they get together. In other words church should be exciting. The Church should become the trend setter not follower, leader not the led, and have exciting music, vibrant praise, creative worship. How exciting is your music? Is it dead? Or from a bygone age? How vibrant is your praise? How creative is the worship? Is it the same old stuff or is it more than that, motivated by a constant pressure to move on and be creative?

Young people will want to be in a church that is alive, creative, vibrant, one that sets trends, challenges, moves constantly, and is willing to live in constant change. Such a group of people are attractive to be with, fun to work with, and a challenge to stay with. The first stop to attracting, training and releasing young people is a live church.

Chapter 2

Challenge

I was driving through London recently, listening to the radio, and I discovered I was tuned into a discussion programme concerning teen violence on the streets. The secular presenter said, "The tragedy of this generation in the west is that no-one is challenging these young people in discovery, belief or cause." I also listened to a man who had been a Student Union President in the 60's. He said that when he was a student there were sit-ins, strikes, and protest marches, but they were all for things like "Ban the Bomb", "Save Biafra", and "Troops out of Vietnam".

He went on to say that in the late 80's and 90's, there are still protests, sit-ins and marches but now they are for causes like "Not enough parking spaces for students cars", "The prices in the refectory are too high", "More money for student grants", and "We should not pay poll tax". Whatever the rights and wrongs of the individual causes are, there does

seem to be a definite shift away from the problems of others such as Biafra and Vietnam and towards those affairs that affect them personally.

One newspaper man also said that this is now a brat age, the age in which children in the west grow up with an expectation that most, if not all, should be provided for them.

Parts of the report are correct, though of course not wholly so. It does illustrate however a delicate shift in our society.

Now I do know that what all young people need is a challenge. It's nice to have high wages, it's nice to drive good cars, live in comfortable homes, have a good education and profitable careers. But frankly, without the challenge of something to live, work, and die for, what is the point of it all? We need to present to young people the challenge of the Gospel of Jesus Christ. This is something to really live for, to be stretched by. There is a whole needy world out there to speak to, to help bring into the greatest Kingdom that ever was or will be. This is a purpose to live for and, if need be, to die for. Jesus is worth it!

If we fail to deliver that challenge we will fail to attract, train and release. The challenge must, I repeat **must**, make demands – demands of commitment, demands of holiness, demands of character development and demands that the cost be paid. If we do not make these demands, not only will we find that we failed to attract, train or release, worse than that, we will have robbed them of the most valuable thing in life, a reason to fight for, a reason to to die for, a reason to exist, in fact, the reason to live!

Chapter 3

Giving Real Responsibility

Ed Cole was saying, in a lecture to men, that the problem of unemployment seems to create a major malaise, in that it causes depression, despondency, a feeling of uselessness, in fact it is a total waste of human resources. He went on to say how so many churches produce exactly the same response from people, for in so many churches 75% of the congregation have nothing to do and no real responsibility. No wonder people get frustrated. Surely the plan of the head for the body was not that it sits in seats to listen to one man? 75% in some churches might be quite good, because I reckon the unemployed in some churches numbers 99%, or near that, with the "one man show" syndrome.

Recently I was in a meeting where the leaders were discussing using young people and their need to be involved, and the fact that leaders need to make it happen. One senior leader from a large church said how he had now got it worked out for his church and was beginning to give real responsibility to young people. He said he was getting them to give out books, take the offering, and to stand on the door when people arrive. Tragically, he was serious. Of course it is necessary to ascertain that young people are willing to take on the small jobs, which can create stability and are part of character development, but that should not be where delegation stops.

Why is it that we so easily forget that Jesus was only 33 years old when he went to the cross? The early apostles were probably in their late 20's at the most, some probably had only just got there. There is the tendency in most churches of all ilks where age becomes the criterion of knowing and doing anything.

If you want to attract, train and release young people in your church you will have to start discovering how you can give real responsibility to these people, not a pretence of responsibility like giving out books, but real responsibility, the sort you would expect to have yourself. Not all in one go, but not waiting until they are pensionable either. We need to move sharply in this area to avoid frustration and disillusionment. Even in many newer churches, particularly those who have worship groups, so often the age group is getting older and there seems to me to be very little effort to use younger people, or in other words, push down the age scale.

Is it too much to ask if there are no teens that could be brought into those groups? I would say we should be looking for good 14 year olds to be ministering in these areas. We need to be training young people as quickly as possible, and letting them have responsibility leading house groups, worship, outreach, church planting etc., etc. They will need support, of course, but remember, most people do more than *they* thought they could, because someone *else* thought they could.

Now is the time to give real responsibility to young people, so they may be developed, released and cause us all to grow.

Chapter 4

Truth and Reality

So often in church life we have in the past lived in unreality. Let's pray that it is changing, and may this small book make a contribution towards the change.

The thing that turns teenagers off quicker than anything is deception, pretence, and a general lack of reality. Today's youth live in a world of many confusions and they want things that are tangible. I don't mean materially tangible but principles to live by, philosophies that work. So often the church has been guilty of answering questions that no-one is asking, making unimportant things important, pretending that important issues don't matter, saying one thing and doing another.

I have often seen churches pay lip-service to evangelism but not really do anything about it, yet just try and move a table that has always stood in one place to another place, and see the fuss and commotion it causes! That is unreality.

It will not do for the Elders to sing and pray like saints in a service and act like the devil at home. That is not truth. It is the number one way to lose youth.

We cannot say we believe in the priesthood of all believers but not allow our children to participate in the real life of the church.

It is impossible to teach, "*Love your enemies*," and then react violently at the first perceived injustice to our person.

We cannot continue to talk about treasures in Heaven that are more valuable than anything else, but then live as if the house and the car are really the only things that matter.

The unthinkable is that we say Jesus is relevant and the answer to the modern world, but continue in our church life to have the trappings, traditions and attitudes from the 18th, 17th, or 16th centuries, and place enormous importance on them.

We must learn to differentiate between the doctrine of God and the traditions of men. One can never be changed; the other is always changing.

I was with a team in a church once. They had had many prayer meetings for revival and for God to move in their town. The team and I were there for a week of outreach and evangelism to the local community. We knew that the church had been praying. The leaflets were printed, the posters were out, we visited, talked, knocked on doors, but the week passed without a breakthrough. Only the faithful, that is the people who were already in the church, came. They talked of blessing, encouragement, the moving of God. Frankly, I was bitterly disappointed.

I wanted to see people saved, added to the church, the Kingdom extended. To me we hadn't achieved, succeeded, or reached that which we came to see.

On the last night, almost as we came to the end of the final service, our hard work with a local group of teenagers paid off. About 30 or 40 of them came to the building to see what we were doing, to sort out who we were, to see if there were any answers. They were not particularly unruly, though they dressed somewhat differently to the present congregation. They also sat on the chairs the wrong way round. It seemed it was easier to listen that way. You could lean on the back and concentrate, you see. There was a near riot from the existing congregation. "These chairs shouldn't be sat on like that! They shouldn't come here dressed like that!!" The Pastor, an "old man" of only 21 years said he'd have to leave early, it was bath night, and would we lock up? That was not church, it was something else. It was dishonest. They did not care that people were lost. I don't care how many hours they had prayed about it, it was total unreality, and I didn't make this story up. Unfortunately I have seen similar happenings in many churches who claim to be praying and to be based on the Great Commission.

If we are to have truth and reality then it must be that we are ourselves all the time. It must be that our programmes are flexible. It must be that what we do is meaningful to those we seek to reach. It must be that we care and love reality in the prayer meeting and outside it. It must be that we will do everything we can to win people to Jesus.

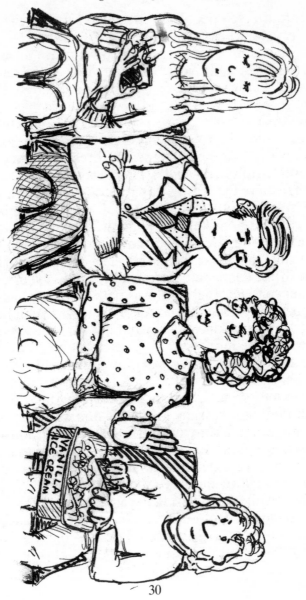

"Well really! I never put my tithe in anything less than a velvet bag."

Chapter 5

Away With Hypocrisy

Walk in the light, as He is in the light. Jesus walked on water and we call it a miracle. We are called to walk in the light and for most of us this is an even greater miracle. Light walking is not an easy matter. In our work place the pressure is on for us to conform, not totally into darkness, but at least to move into the shadows.

At school, at play, in our family life, even in the church, there is pressure on from the world to conform to move into shadow land. A small lie. A small theft. A pretence in church that wouldn't hold water at home where they really know us. I'm always suspicious when people are pressing others into the shadows. I know a man who said to a young Christian, "Well now, you need to spend at least one half-hour at the beginning of each day in prayer." His wife embarassingly said out loud for all the company to hear, "But you don't do that." That is shadow land.

Jesus was so embarassingly open. He wept, He was

31

angry, He said He was tired. He ate with unclean hands. He called Pharisees hypocrites. He talked to prostitutes. Jesus broke social customs whenever they got in the way of the Father's business. What He always did was to walk in the light. He is the light. By the way, "walking in the light" does not mean giving all your enemies the answers, like some Christians seem to think. Jesus often refused to answer or simply evaded an answer by posing his own question. "Walking in the light" means being a self revealer, especially in relationships where trust is involved such as with leaders, husband and wife, in the home and in our general lives. It does not mean revealing all to every person we meet or know casually. Jesus said He did not reveal Himself to man because He knew what was in man and He knew that their hearts were deceitful.

"Walking in the light" means being consistent at home and in the church. It means keeping promises to wives, husbands and children. It means we need to be the same off the platform as on. It means that we will take the risk that some we have trusted our lives and secrets with will let us down. Jesus chose to reveal Himself to Judas Iscariot. It means that our children won't say, "but my father and mother are different at home to what they are in church." It means we will not play the pretence game, it means we will be attractive to others, particularly to youth who hate sham and hypocrisy, even though they sometimes show it. It means we will be light walkers.

Chapter 6

Listen – Talk – Affirm

Dr. Donald Howard suggests in his book *To Change a Nation*, that if we really think about it, children do more things right than they do wrong. The problem is that we notice the wrong more clearly than the right. Are we listening or even noticing properly?

The definition of a bore is a person who speaks when I want to. The art of attracting, training and releasing is first of all to listen seriously, and then to listen carefully, and then to listen. So often you see parents who don't listen to their children, teachers who don't listen to their students, leaders who don't listen to those who are following.

Listening does not always assume that the speaker is correct in what they say. It does assume that you respect them, value them and are willing to hear.

So often with youth and young teens we assume (if we are older) that their job is always to listen to us.

"Sorry to bother you pastor but. . . ."

"Ah Joe. I've been meaning to talk to you about giving up smoking. I really feel . . ."

"I only wanted to tell you my friend Pete has just become a Christian."

Not so. If we do not listen they will never hear us. One day my young son (aged 10 at the time) phoned me from where he was staying with relatives for a few days. He said, "Dad, I just phoned you to give you a word of advice". He went on, "I think you should do so and so in the church." I listened carefully, thanked him and have acted on his advice up to this point in time.

Learn to listen to your children and young people.

Talk, that's a two way conversation. It involves listening as well as speaking. We run day schools and there are often staff who are having problems with students. They have tried all sorts of things to bring correction, but without success. My advice is usually, "Take them out to McDonalds and buy them a milkshake and sit and chat". Those who have tried my cure often find that it does work. It not only works for teacher and student, it will also work for parent and child or parent and teenager. A Mcdonalds milkshake is not a magic cure-all-ills; it is taking time to talk.

Isn't it strange how we all tend to emphasise the negative? We notice what is wrong, we pay little attention to what is right. We are usually better on correction that we are on congratulation, more astute at criticism than confirmation, showing the pitfalls by our advice to teenagers rather than acclamation, complaining of the problems that go with opportunities, rather than looking for opportunities to give affirmation.

We need to learn to strengthen the right rather than just simply knock the wrong. We need to learn to look for the good and affirm it. We need to learn to constantly encourage those areas of good ideas, good actions, good habits and good intentions. Note it, approve it, affirm it. It will make strong people in the end.

Chapter 7

Visibility

When I first came to London and joined the church at Finsbury Park I was told that, sadly, there were no youth in the church. At my first service I noted a row of young people. At the end I went to them presuming that, like me, they were newcomers. "Are you visiting this area?" I asked. "Oh no, we have been in the church for years" was their reply.

My assumption, and in fact my discovery, is that when young people grow up in a church community the steps from 5 years old to 15 years old take place so imperceptibly that they tend to get overlooked. What happens is that their presence becomes like a piece of well-loved, unused furniture, standing in the same place, not noticed when moved, or worse, stolen. Young people just blend into the background.

We need to take positive, conscious steps in church life to make ourselves notice that our young people are growing up quickly. We should not treat a 14 year old like an 8 year old and a 7 year old should be treated with respect.

A major attraction for youth is youth. What an obvious statement, yet to make that obvious in action we must make those young people visible.

That visibility can take place in a training mode, such as leading worship. The youth will then from time to time be visible on the platform. Most worship groups get older and older by the year and fail to push the age down and add in new blood.

They could be trained as house group leaders. Make them a deputy leader somewhere. That will mean giving them visibility in the house group and from time to time real responsibility.

They could be trained to preach. That will mean giving them visibility on your platform, because all theory and no practice does not work and is not good enough.

They could be trained in teaching, then you will have to give them visibility as teachers.

They could be trained to prophesy, pray for the sick, minister in words of knowledge and wisdom, but of course as you train them in these areas, you must give them opportunity to work in these areas, and that will increase their visibility.

Some churches have very good training programmes, but the best training programmes fail, because training without work-related experience is not only a waste of time, energy and resources, it is positively dangerous. Dangerous? Yes, for it leads to a build-up of power, a build up of ability, which at best, if not utilised, will lead to frustration and at worst, if not used, will lead to a total explosion, a blow-up, a wrecking of lives. I wonder why we don't give the visibility necessary in our churches?

The usual answers are that they are too young, they lack experience, one day perhaps, the older ones won't listen, their time will come. I wonder how old the disciples were, I wonder how much we feel threatened by the youth, by their talents and abilities.

If you want to attract, train and release, then you will have to find ways of giving visibility, which entails giving responsibility and of course, training.

If you don't want to attract, train and release, I guess you will carry on waiting until they get older, when you'll probably lose them.

Chapter 8

Opportunities

If you have only got one young person in your church, there is potential, there is possibility. Supposing you see the young man is going to make a preacher. You can, of course, begin to open doors of opportunity to exercise his gifts. You may ask him, for example, to help you lead the service once a month. You may as he progresses ask him to preach once in a while. You could take him with you (you *should* take him with you) and expose him to other areas of the work of God. All good and right.

However, what do you do if you have got 10 such young people or 20 or 50? Are you going to give all 50 an opportunity once every 6 weeks? Or I suppose you could send them off to Bible College, or away on some ministry team, although this will mean that they have never had the opportunity to learn the basics in their home environment, in their home situation amongst people who really know them. Instead they have to be thrown in amongst strangers, with very little basic knowledge, and maybe as a very young Christian.

So what am I advocating? Church growth has been much discussed these last 10 years or so. We have seen, or some have, the need to reach this generation with the good news that Jesus Christ is alive and wants to befriend people. Alongside this we need growth for the sake of the world out there. One of the ways that growth is achieved is in the training and development of young people.

It is the duty of the leadership to create openings and opportunities for ministry. Constantly, leadership should be asking: How can I train this one to lead? How can I train that one to preach? How can I develop this youngster's prophetic gift? How can I teach this one to be an effective counsellor? How can I develop that one's gift to administrate? How do I develop some of these youngsters into apostles? Under God, we should be seeking to do all this, and more.

Theoretical training is necessary, but theory without practice and practical training is a very poor substitute. Yes, it will put pressure on you to find new areas, to constantly look for ways of giving opportunities for these young people to minister. We need to attract, train and release. Give opportunities at the right level, opportunities that afford possibilities of development, opportunities that are progressive. From my experience this policy, when functioning, will result in growth in the church across the board. Opportunities given to youth creates growth and more opportunities.

"Due to his unfortunate accident last Sunday, the organist is not playing this morning."

44

Chapter 9

Experimentation

Isn't it strange how Christians often seem to be so afraid of experimentation? We can see this in the so called "professional ministry" by the clothes that they wear. They were once the traditional dress of the day, but because of the resistance to change them, it became an unalterable way of dressing. Doesn't it seem strange to you how some churches keep on doing the same things, even though it is obvious they are not working?

I remember 10 years ago when, as one of the leadership in North London, I began to make radical changes in the structure of the church, the people church that is, and even in the way we used the buildings. Some of the other leaders said to me, "Why do we need all these changes? What right do we have to experiment?"

My answer never changed, "we must change what is not working, what is not bringing the desired results, what is not actually effective in producing growth in the Church of God."

This was usually countered with, "But, maybe your experiment will be wrong too." My answer to that is, "Yes, that may be so, but we don't know that yet. What we do know is that the status quo is not working, so better to experiment and perhaps make a new mistake, with a possibility of success, than stick with the old mistake, which we have proved is failing."

One Pentecostal Pioneer, Percy Brewster, said something that certainly helped me as a youngster in the midst of experimental confrontation with those who were older and should have been wiser. He said, "The Doctrine of God never changes: the traditions of men can always be changed and often should be. The problem is, most Christians do not know the difference between doctrine and tradition."

Perhaps that desire to hang on to traditions, the determination not to change, stems from the knowledge that God is the unchanging one. Well he is, of course, the same yesterday and today and forever. But I'm not God, neither is the way we do things God. God does not change in His character, but as the Creator he never seems to do things the same way twice.

Never are two snowflakes the same. Never are two blades of grass matched. Never are two people, not even identical twins, clones. Never are there two fingerprints that match. Never are two sets of DNA structures alike.

Dare we say, never are two revivals just the same. Never are two local churches perfectly matched. I'm sure I could go on but that's not my style.

Experiment! is my plea. If the doctrine is sound, the application can always change, and often needs to change. Isn't it wonderful how the Bible deals with principles rather than with specifics, leaving us to take the principles and apply them to a multiplicity of situations in ever changing ways?

Experimentation for young people (the right experiment) is both necessary and valuable. The ways of approach will be different, the ways of doing things will be different. Do we have the right to defend a position that is not getting results, that is obviously not reaching our world with the Good News? Do not then let them have a go their way, with counselling, help, advice, encouragement, but never, please never with the standard clichés – "But that's the way we have always done it" or "We've never done it that way before".

To attract train and release, our approach to our youth should now be, "You may be doing it totally different to how we would do it. It may be 100% more effective than the way we do it, or it may not, but under God, we allow you the priviledge of trying this experiment, of reaching out into new spheres, of doing what we have never done." Who knows, maybe their new ideas are the Holy Spirit's answers to the now?

Chapter 10

The Clash of Methods

How quickly the traditions of men become the "doctrines of God." Of course the traditions are not God's doctrine, plan or way; it's just that we want to make them so.

The problem is perceived, or at least comes to the surface, when young people start to do things. Whatever they do, whether its praise and worship, evangelism, leading house groups, leisure activity, work, preaching, leading meetings, whatever, we are going to have problems, because methodology is constantly changing. The way those who are older did it has now changed, and when you look at the youngsters do it, the irritations overwhelm. The older ones' response is often, "you can't do it that way, we never did it that way, we have been doing it this way for years, whats wrong with our way of doing it? Why don't you do it our way? We are experts in this and this is the way to do it."

If all these arguments fail we sometimes go on to

say, "God doesn't want it done that way". The young person may question, "how do you know?", to which we reply, "We are older, know better, have been on the way longer, you need to respect our way, our tradition", and on and on and on.

When I first came to London the church wanted to reach out to the local community, particularly to reach the young people. Instead of running the show I said to a group of the youngsters in the fellowship, "here's the budget, here is the room you can use, we want to reach young people in the area." The first thing they did was to change the lighting in that room. Suddenly there were coloured bulbs everywhere. The music became relevant and upbeat, and the older members of the church at that time wanted my head on a plate. Why? Well they said it was "worldly" and they "hadn't done it that way before" and "that wasn't the way evangelism was done in the past". One lady thought the coloured lights introduced too much pomp and ceremony into what she described as a previously "free church". I'm not sure quite what she meant by "free".

The truth is we don't have a monopoly on the best method. The message doesn't change, the emphasis does. The truth doesn't change, but methods of presentation do. God doesn't change, but how well we know Him does. Sin is sin, but people's perception of it will change. Television, the arts, communication, media, politics, car phones, high rise flats, all will have an effect on our methods.

So, all in all, we can see what a problem most of us face when it comes to understanding someone else's methods. The roots lie in our traditions and our unwillingness to change and our lack of perception that there is a possibility of a better way.

The results will not always justify the means, and unrighteous methods which apparently bring success are nevertheless unacceptable. However, we must be careful how quickly we jump to say, wrong! ungodly! unrighteous! We must first take a good look at our insecurities and fears and be honest with ourselves about our resistance to change. We need to know what causes us to react the way we do.

We must give time and space to ourselves as well as those we are training, in order to see clearly, check results and find out about the quality of what is being produced by new methods. A "stand back, watch and see" approach will not always hurt us, and whilst it's true that we often need to steer, input and guide, we also need to allow others (or our Youth) real responsibility, freedom and flexibility, enveloped in acceptancy of their new methods.

I am confident you will be pleasantly surprised how often something so different can work, and bring glory to God.

Chapter 11

Believing

"Most people can do more than they thought they could do, because somebody else thought they could do it." So says Dr. Donald Howard.

"It is impossible for anyone to live under continual disapproval", says Gerald Coates.

We all need others who believe in us. We need to believe in our children and in our young people. We need to appreciate them, value them, and make sure they know that and understand their worth to us. Most times we are all too slow to congratulate and appreciate. Let us do much better in that area. Conversely, we are all too quick to correct, reprimand and admonish. We criticise and nag when things are wrong.

I have discovered that more people don't believe in themselves than do. Most people can be persuaded to rise way above what they are doing when you begin to trust what they are doing. We need to stretch people for their benefit, our benefit and the benefit of the Kingdom. Stretching causes growth, stretching causes maturity, stretching releases people. To stretch someone you have to trust them beyond the point where they are performing at the moment. To stretch someone you will need to believe in them. That causes them to believe in themselves, and even more importantly it throws them so often back into the strength, wisdom, development, power and production of the fruit of the Spirit which only God can bring. He wants us stretched. He has a goal in mind for us. He plans that we shall be conformed to the image of His Son and if that's not stretching, nothing is.

In many churches that I have been to, people start by telling you what they have not got. It's a usual human problem you can see again and again in the scriptures.

Elijah goes to the widow of Nain and asks,

"What have you got?"

"Nothing", she replies.

Her second reply is,

"Nothing except a little meal and oil."

"Good," says the prophet, "Give it to me."

When she had given her last she discovered she had enough to sustain them all.

The widow of the prophet in 2 Kings 4 comes to Elisha and says,

"My sons will be sold into slavery to pay my bills."

"What have you got?" he asks.

"Nothing" is her first reply.

"A little oil" is her second.

"It's God's will to stretch you."

Given in faith to God, it is all that is necessary.

"Feed the people," Jesus says.

"How?" asks the disciples.

"What have you got?"

"Nothing" is their first reply.

"Five loaves and two small fishes" is the second.

"Bring them to me."

They then became sufficient to feed five thousand men plus women and children. When God gives us something to do, our usual response to Him is to ask, "With what shall we do it?" When we look at the size of the task and the resources available we are well prepared for God's next question to us. "What have you got?"

"Nothing", is the reply.

But we need to think again, because He is asking again, and we need to perhaps say, "A few young people, not mature enough, not developed enough, not old enough." Give them to Him, for broken in His hands they will be sufficient to do the task that is ahead. You see, God believes in them.

Why not, God believes in you!

Chapter 12

Peer Group Responsibility

This one needs to be prayed for. It is always more difficult to lead a group when you have never been part of the group. Not impossible, just harder.

That's why I reckon that this area, especially, needs to be prayed for. In the end it is the Holy Spirit who calls leadership and gives gifts to the Church. It's the Church's responsibility to recognise it and release it.

Whenever you see a group on the corner of the street, I guarantee one of them is a leader. They need to be captured for God. Something special happens in a group when one of their own gets switched on and begins to believe, and, from God's point of view, to go in the right direction. They may have to suffer a period of ridicule, extra pressure, teasing or just for a while, ostracism, but something is happening. A metamorphosis is taking place in that group and fairly rapidly. For most of the group there will be a new respect, a new willingness to listen, a desire to follow, a secret pleasure that he or she is one of us, and "look at them now".

The same thing happens in a church fellowship when God calls. It's great when the natural leader of the youngsters in the church emerges and is one of the youngsters. It will have a far greater effect on the whole group. Now direction is coming from one of their own. Now vision is coming from one of their own, now methodology is coming from one of their own. Therefore it's easier for all to respond, to follow, to get on board. From the church point of view its far more effective, as the leadership is not imposed from above. The leadership is one of their own, and the youngsters relate to the leader in terms of "He's one of us". This all makes for a more rapidly integrated push forward, by a greater number of people. It's peer-group responsibility/leadership and it is the most effective way. We need to pray that God will help us to unearth this kind of person and that He will commission them.

Perhaps at this time quite a lot of support will need to be given to the emerging leader from other more mature (notice I didn't say older) leaders. One of the things that will help is the recognition by mature and older leaders of this new leader. This will assist them in leading the group, bringing about stability, getting new leaders, holding them, and releasing into that peer group new areas of ministry that have not been seen before. A new era of opportunity will begin to take place.

We should never be afraid to experiment in these areas, even if we sometimes fail. Most failure is not the end of the world, even though some of us think it is. If God gives you these developing leaders within peer groups, you are in for good things, so don't suppress them. Carefully develop them and seek for greater release. Their understanding and effectiveness will be far greater than any imported or imposed youth leader.

"Teddy adds a real secure dimension to my life."

Chapter 13

Move Up

Isn't it strange the things we use to build up our confidence, and the things we hang on to to give us a feeling of value and usefulness?

God thinks we are most valuable. He believes that we are a pearl of great price. For that reason He has paid the highest price possible to get us. He gave His only Son to get us. The death of Christ on the cross was to purchase us. He considers us most valuable, highly priced, the peak, yet we so often fail to realise that.

Instead we try to find a value in our usefulness. What this often means in practice, especially in church life, is that we hold on to tasks given us, because that way we feel useful and somehow it justifies our worth. We don't admit to it, of course, but that's what is happening. It also happens with secular jobs, which is why redundancy and unemployment are so debilitating. What we do gives us value. If we could understand this fact, the real truth is that what we *are* is what is truly valuable. Therefore what we do becomes an expression of what we are, and what we should be is continually developing.

This humanistic, wrong teaching, usually causes a loss of people, particularly youth. What happens is this. Someone has a gift of leading worship, so the leadership asks him to do it. He does it well, feels valuable, feels wanted, needed and useful, which of course he is. Then as time passes, there are other young people who get saved and join the fellowship. In time it is discovered that their gifting, their ability, their know-how is greater than his. But now we have a problem, how to use the new talent. This is not easy. He is in position and is not easily going to allow anyone to muscle in on his job. He makes a pretence of co-operation, but inside himself he is being awkward, resistent, and generally finding many reasons for not doing anything that would help these new ones to develop. Why should he? Inside him there is the voice of inferiority saying, "If they do it, they might be better, what will I do, what will I be needed for?" So he hangs on, he resists and in the upcoming youngsters is built total frustration which could lead to explosion and loss. So there has been a complete failure to train and release. Does this happen in your fellowship? Look carefully.

What should happen is that he should becomes a developer, an encourager, a teacher, an enabler. He should quickly move, not to a point of unemployment, not to a point of sitting doing nothing, not to a point of uselessness, not to a point of disability, but move nevertheless.

First, he should move to help the new ones get established, not to do it his way, but to develop their own way and style. Secondly, he should gradually pass more and more responsibility over to them. Thirdly, at the same time he should be seeking God to either move over to areas that were not being covered by the fellowship properly, or develop ministries that still are not being filled in the church. We need to realise that what God wants is our development. He wants to move us on up. To make us become ten-talent people rather than one-talent people. He wants us to become daring, inventive, creative people, like Him.

If he had perceived that his real value was not what he does but who he is, he would discover greater things, new things, new possibilities that God has in store for him. He would discover that he had become more useful, more valuable, that not only is he, as a person, being developed, but that the whole church is being taken on further as he is being used by God to make it happen, and as a further blessing, he will have been instrumental in attracting, training and releasing.

Chapter 14

Heroes

Clay feet are what we discover heroes have when we get older and more mature. At least for most of us that is what happens, but we did have heroes. I'm sure you will acknowledge that all children and teens go through a hero stage.

The Bible says that as a man thinks, so he is. What we see on TV, read and hear is what goes into our mind and therefore what we think. Surely those we adopt as heroes, at whatever age, will strongly affect our thinking.

Having heroes seems to be a little-understood concept by anyone past the age of 22. Yet almost all of us had heroes for some period of our life. The teenage heroes are many, pop idols, sports stars, imaginary super saviours for children. The hero is someone who they really want to know about. What food do they eat? Where do they live? What is their favourite colour? From these trivia they move on to understand things like what is their lifestyle?

What is their value system? What is important to my hero?

The natural progression from there is to adopt the hero's standards. Their favourite colour becomes ours, we want to copy their lifestyle, and their value system becomes our value system. This will apply if the hero system is drawn from the drug culture, from the materialistic society or whatever sub-culture they are into.

Children's comic publishers have realised how strong the influence of heroes is and so are trying to act responsibly. They point out the fact that Superman is a non-smoker, recognising how powerful that message is coming from the hero. Unfortunately most heroes who are accessible to our young people do not care about the morals of those who follow. They are often only interested in propagating an offensive, destructive lifestyle, one that will destroy, break down, and bring them to nothing.

Isn't it strange how the enemy of human beings, the devil, uses a Biblical strategy to persuade people? He uses heroes, he makes disciples, he recognises the desire of people to follow others. I believe the subject of heroes is one that has been neglected in the Church, particularly with our young people. There shouldn't be a deficiency, for there are heroes a-plenty, starting with the heroes of Hebrews, moving on to the makers of Church history, the Christian revolutionaries of the ages and on to the heroes of social change. Britain has had more than her fair share of people like that, – those who started hospitals, freed slaves, fed the poor, cared for orphans and they are not all dead.

There are Christian heroes alive today. Our age has had the biggest group of non-heroes ever, however, there are still real, live, Christian heroes. Sell those heroes to your young people, talk them up, give them positive alternatives, show them people who really are to be admired, whose lifestyle, value system and goals we like and would love others to adopt. It can happen. It will happen.

To encourage Christian heroes we need to give them a high profile, inform our youngsters about those leaders we admire, and encourage others to want to be like them. The great heroes of the past need to be presented so that we may copy and follow them. It will take imagination to work it out, sometimes the correction of our humanistic teaching as to how small a part Christian heroes played in the world's development. They did not play a small part; it was large and significant, from the abolition of slavery to the change in employment laws. Right across the gamut of all social action, Christian heroes are still leading the way. At the time of writing it is a Christian organisation led by Christians that is having the greatest impact on the AIDS crisis (ACET). The heroes are there, but we need to give a high profile of them to our youngsters.

Paul says, *Follow me, as I also follow hard after Christ*. There are great heroes in the Church. We need to talk them up and show them to others, particularly our young, impressionable, up-and-coming youth. They need the heroes who will attract them.

It is possible for them to have such heroes; make sure they are aware of them. These heroes will help us in our attracting, training and releasing.

Chapter 15

Friend

We have to make rules and regulations, don't we? Isn't it strange how we have taken the reconciliation of God by his son, Jesus, and turned it into a religion? We have taken such statements as: "*I no longer call you servant, but friend*" and we have turned it into rules and regulations. Christianity is not a religion, never has been, and never will be. Christianity is about relationships. Relationship with God the Son, and communion, or constant communication, with God the Holy Spirit. Relationships are stimulating and fun. You can try to put rules around them, but that will always end up spoiling the relationship.

Good relationships are loving and caring, and we respond to them out of love and respect for the other person, not because someone tells us to. That might mean we continually do the same thing over and over again, and to the non-discerning onlooker, it seems like a rule. Let me illustrate with a story.

For a while I had a foster daughter. One day I was

aware that she planned to go to a particular party and I did not want her to, not because I am against parties, but I was concerned about this one, mainly because of some of the people I knew would be present. So now what to do? First of all I stated my case; that wasn't heard. So what next, maybe an argument? Then I hit on the plan. I explained that as we were friends, and as she was 17 years old, it was really not right for me to say she could not go to this party, however it would really hurt me if she did, even though we would still be friends. She didn't go to the party. When I was surprised enough to ask why, I was told eagerly, "Because I didn't want to upset my friend, even though I wanted to go. My friend is more important".

Law can get things done, but it never really solves things long term. Things are so much better when our hearts are in it. The opposite story could be told of the little boy, who was asked by his Dad to sit at the table. His answer was "No!". After remonstrations Dad, being stronger than junior, put his hand on his son's shoulder and pushed him into the sitting position at the table. Junior then spoke up, "I may be sitting down on the outside, but inside I'm standing up."

No wonder God says He wants our hearts. When the heart responds in friendship and love, rules are unnecessary. "The law is for the lawless"-and perhaps the friendless.

Chapter 16

Coffee and Ice Cream

I believe, and I'm sure you do too, that what we do is as important as what we say, and how we say it makes it valid or invalid. Then how come our reprimands to our children and teenagers are often so lacking in thought? Usually, from my observations, reprimands and corrections are often bad-tempered affairs. But like most things, to do it well, takes time.

The Bible tells me various things about discipline, both to one another and with our children. It tells us to rebuke in love, which must surely mean that I have the other person's best interests at heart. It means I will thoughtfully choose my words, and I will choose the right opportunity, which won't usually (although I wouldn't say never) take place in the middle of a room full of people. In a rebuke sometimes hard things have to be said, which should not be ducked, but require the best opportunity I can make.

In terms of the discipline of children, the Bible tells us that we must not break the spirit of the child. The

"Do you add anything to your coffee and ice cream? You always look so happy."

child must be disciplined in such a way as to bring the will under control, but not cower or break the determination to enquire, develop and succeed.

The Bible further states that fathers should not provoke their children to wrath. I'm sure that there are things we can do which will provoke, such as nag, seem to be unreasonable, not explain why discipline is necessary, not lay clear rules, or not uphold the rules we have laid down. Often children do things by accident. Our reaction to an accident, if we are Godly people, will be entirely different to our reaction to a disobedient act. The disobedient act, no matter how small, is always more serious than an accident, no matter how great. Often that is not the way we react.

I have noticed, particularly with teenage children, and also with some teachers, that there is almost a tendency to discipline in such a way that makes the teenager feel small and not yet adult. Being made to look foolish in front of your peers is not a successful way to get co-operation, nor is it usually a loving or profitable approach. Teenagers want to feel adult. There are times when they act in a very adult fashion and there are other times when they act younger than their years. Why not appeal to their adult side and reprimand privately whenever possible, even though I know that isn't always possible? Remember, the purpose of disciplining a person is to teach them to discipline themselves, when you are not there, or as Dr. Donald Howard would say, "Discipline is not what you do *to* a person it is what you do *for* a person."

So what has all this to do with coffee and ice cream, which is the title of this chapter? Well it's just that it is my firm belief that a great deal can be done to further attracting, training and releasing young people, if parents, teachers, pastors and leaders who have to deal with teenage problems by discipline, confrontation and general advice, would take the person they are seeking to guide out for a talk and a good listen. In Britain a good way is over a cup of coffee and perhaps an ice cream. For me I reckon coffee and ice cream works wonders!

Chapter 17

Drawing Lines

Two men arrived one day at the foot of a rather dangerous mountain. They wanted to conquer it and go right to the top. This was the aim of them both. The first got his tackle, said he was happy doing it himself, he knew what he was doing, and went off to climb. The second hired his tackle, but he also asked in the small town, who was the very best guide on this mountain. They found the guide and he hired him too. The second man always referred to the guide, conquered the mountain and returned safely to base. The first man never reached the top and his body was taken off by a mountain rescue team less than half way up. Which of these men do you think was free to climb the mountain?

Freedom is not an absence of restrictions or controls. In fact true freedom can only be seen in the context of laws that are laid down for the safety of all.

When we draw lines from a loving heart for young people, or for that matter any people, we are not

"Oh come off it Dad! That's drawing the line a bit harsh . . . it's hardly fashionable!"

taking away freedom. We are not even laying down a law that may never be changed, adjusted or modified. What we are doing is drawing a line for that person and for others. We are building security, confidence and stability. We are giving a frame of reference in which to work and to live. That is a very helpful thing to do.

One evening one of my daughters asked permission to go to a party. My answer was "yes". I was pacing up and down quite worried at 1.30 a.m. in the morning as I still had no daughter home. When the door opened, I sprang into action. "What time do you call this?"

"It's half past one dad", was the reply.

"That's very late."

"Well, yes but it was a party and you didn't say that I had to be back at any specific time."

The failure to draw a line had caused me my own problem. It is not good enough to say, "you should have known, you knew you shouldn't have done that." For future occasions we drew very clearly defined and agreed lines and encountered very few problems.

Many leaders and families are afraid to draw lines, feeling somehow it's old fashioned and unacceptable in the 90's. In reality, whatever age we live in, such lines help us to live well.

I believe that drawing lines for children and teens will be a positive step forward in attracting, training and releasing youth into their full potential. When we draw the lines they must be reasonable. Crossing over the lines must be dealt with, but again in a reasonable manner. The lines must be clear, and that does not just mean clear to the line-drawer but clear to the person whose life the line affects. It is also essential that the line should in most cases, but not all, be an agreed line. It is also essential that the person for whom the line is drawn understands why the line is drawn there, what are the perceived benefits, and that there may well be a change in the line's position in the future depending on circumstances, attitudes and action.

To quote Dr. Donald Howard again, "The right reaction towards a responsibility should in the end lead to a greater freedom and flexibility. On the other hand, a wrong reaction to a responsibility should lead to restricted freedom and flexibility." Happy line drawing!

Chapter 18

Discipline With Respect

The younger you start the better. In this book we are talking about youth and how to attract them, train them and release them into fulfilling lives, and I would hope effective ministry in the Kingdom of God. However, it is still true to say that the younger you start, the better and in fact easier, it will be. As one proverb says "It's better to build children than to repair people" If we get the foundations right, the building on top will be sound.

It is important that we start as young as possible, particularly if the psychologists are right who say, "A child's character and disposition is set, as if in concrete, by the time it reaches 5 years old"

There seem to me to be two ends to the balance of discipline, and discipline will in the end have an effect on how well you do in attracting, training and releasing. There's the kind of family, church, or school, which almost never disciplines, but always treats everything with what I call misplaced kindness, which is really slushy sentimentality. Kids rule, okay! is the watchword for the family. The children's bedtime, routine, school, leisure, home coming, going-out, takes precedent in the family and in fact, even though many parents would deny that this is happening, the child or children become the hub of life, as everthing revolves around them. That is a wrong position for a child to be in and will only create real problems in later life.

God does not take us into His family and then adjust the family to suit us. He brings pressure to bear that changes us, so that we eventually conform to the image of Christ.

My family, it seems to me, have conformed to my input, so meal times, bed times, going to church times, have had to be brought into line for the family. I'm not saying that a new baby does not cause upheaval and adjustment in a family, but in our western culture we take it far too far and make an unneccesary meal out of it. We turn what should be a pleasure (having children), which is a blessing from God, into a chore and a problem, and it can become a totally constricting experience.

Three children have not constricted my family life, my married life, my social life or my ability to go places, do things, and attend church. In fact my three terrific kids have expanded and enriched every area.

The other side of the discipline spectrum is one where the little infant is so disciplined they become like a coiled spring, fine when parents are around, perfectly behaved when Dad or Mum is in the room, but oh! What a nightmare for everyone else when the child is left alone and the spring is loosed and the child bounces with the wrecking ability of a major demolition company, over everything and everyone! The purpose of discipline is very simple, though often not understood. It is to make you act right when authority is present, so that you learn to act right when authority is absent. It must eventually be part of you.

I started this chapter by saying "discipline with respect." You can see that I believe in discipline, but done the right way. I'm sure that will also include the occasional, and note I say "occasional", spanking. Even so, do it with respect, so there are ground rules for disciplining with respect, such as:

1. Don't discipline when you are in a state of anger – wait until you have cooled down. When you discipline in anger, anger is sown in the child.

2. Don't over-react – you don't or you shouldn't, chop off a man's head for stealing a loaf of bread, for if you do that, what will you do when someone else commits murder?

I have often observed what I consider the "over the top" parent, who grounds a teenager for a month for a small first-time wrong option, when a night in would have been far more appropriate.

3. Don't do it in a way that embarrasses the person in front of a peer group. The exception to that is when a child or teenager has

committed the same offence in the presence of the group, and been disciplined privately. They need to be told "Next time, I will take action in front of your friends, even if it embarrasses you, which I don't want to do". There probably won't be a next time if you have got the rest right.

4. Don't make threats that you can't, or have no intention of keeping. There is nothing more annoying than a person who constantly says, "The next time you do that I will smack you", and the next time the offence is committed, they say again "The next time you do that I will smack you". This form of non-action teaches the person:

    a. That authority is lying.
    b. That authority is insincere.
    c. That the wrongdoing is not important and therefore can be continued.

    So, therefore, non-action reinforces the wrong action. What a mess!

5. Do discipline in love. Actually, if you bring me an undisciplined person, tragically, I will show you an unloved person. God the Father says *Those "Whom I love, I also discipline."* He goes on to say, *"If I didn't discipline you, you would be like a bastard to me."* We are not, of course, we are his children: He is our father and therefore discipline is an indication of His love.

6. Do discern the difference between a mistake and a wrong action. For example if a child knocks a glass off a table and it breaks due to a clumsy action, that's a mistake, and while a remark about being careful may be appropriate, and you are probably upset about the broken glass, discipline is inappropriate. However, if you have previously said, do not throw that ball in here, you might break my glass, and then an act of disobedience takes place and the glass gets broken, that is not a mistake, that is rebellion and discipline becomes appropriate.

7. Do set lines. If people break your rules, but they didn't know it was your rule, that's your fault and not their's. People/children must know, "This is the line you must not cross." Such lines actually bring confidence and enable people to know where they are. Without such a measure we are in uncharted seas and feel lost.

8. Do explain yourself. There is nothing more frustrating than to be disciplined without understanding. Explain and explain again.

9. Do be friends with those you have to discipline. Proverbs says, *"Faithful are the wounds of a friend"*.

10. Do quickly bring restoration and affirmation after discipline. This will strengthen the person and make it all worthwhile, and you will discover you have got, trained and released.

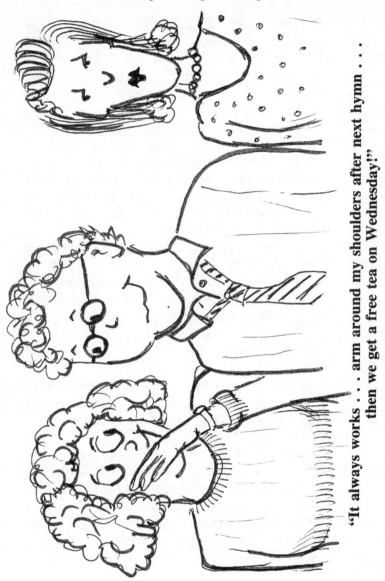

"It always works . . . arm around my shoulders after next hymn . . . then we get a free tea on Wednesday!"

Chapter 19

Marriage Counselling and
Marriage Training

One could wonder what marriage counselling and training has got to do with attracting, training and releasing youth. The fact is, as with discipline, the earlier you start, the greater your chance of success.

Many problems are created in the life of the teenager because of life at home. We are foolish if we cannot see that the 80's and 90's have been to some extent the reaping time for the seeds sown in the 60's.

Weak family life and weak parenting, will create a weak church and problem youth.

I do not believe that marriage and courting is something we don't need teaching about and that we will automatically get it right because it is something that comes naturally. It doesn't come that way; it comes from what we observe in our upbringing, the role models that we had in our mothers and fathers and the atmosphere that was created at home. All that will affect what we are like as we grow up. If those models have been bad ones, then our chance of success in the areas that are important, such as relationships, going on with God, stability etc., will be impaired.

For this reason, as a church, for many years now, we have required our young couples who plan to marry to go through quite an intensive pre-marital training course. This involves 3–7 evenings with another couple we have previously trained, who, through discussion, will help the couple to understand the Biblical perspective on marriage. We cover such things as leaving and cleaving, the use of money, open, honest communication, the Biblical way to argue, plus other subjects, creating a base on which to build a successful family, thus creating fewer problems for their children.

In 16 years of ministry in North London we have not had one divorce in a church that marries roughly 2 couples per month. I wouldn't say that we are doing everything right, or that every marriage is perfect, but it does seem that we are doing something right. There are major upheaval areas in everyone's life, such as going to school, to work, to college, courting/marriage, the first baby, retirement, death. If the church, with its gifts of God, via its leadership and ministries, can be alongside at these points, to help people over the hurdles, a great deal of heartache can be avoided.

As a pre-requisite to marriage, we will, in the Fellowship, keep our eyes open to see those who are getting romantically involved. We would then invite them for a meal or a coffee, and in a friendly natter explain some principles which will enable them to develop a friendship on a good basis and avoid some of the hurts. This will establish a good basis for a future marriage, if that's the way it develops. Some would see these things, perhaps, as interfering; I see them as caring. What it does long term is enable a firm foundation to be put into the family, and thus into the life of the church and the children. The teens that come from these families shouldn't have some of the hangups that have been produced by our one-parent – divorce-orientated – "this relationship is a problem, let's dump it" kind of a society.

Chapter 20

Strong Families

It has always been a source of amazement to me that instructions for Church leadership, as given in 1 Timothy 2, are so universally ignored. I mentioned in my book "Leadership and . . ." the leader who couldn't get his young son to school because his wife wasn't supportive and the young lad would heed no instructions. How then, I asked myself then, and still do now, was he supposed to lead the church?

Surely, before we get others right and give instructions to lead the church in any way, we need to have ourselves under control. We need to have order and togetherness in our own lives, at least within reason. After our personal life comes the family, where it is often the hardest place to be a Christian. Because it's difficult to maintain a pretence or the facade at home, the real us shows all too clearly in how we act and react.

The first step towards having strong families must be to act and react in the home as we do in the

fellowship of believers, and in our work place and during our leisure time. It will save a lot of hard work in the end, because keeping the facade in place is so complicated and requires so much effort, it's much better to relax. That doesn't mean that there won't be adjustments needed. What we are, frequently needs to change. The plan is to be like Christ, and that will require constant change, but at least it will take place in the context of reality rather than pretence.

It seems to me that there is nothing that alienates teenagers more quickly than to observe pretence and hypocrisy in those of us who profess to be adults.

For 15 years I have participated in youth camps of all types. Camping for young people is a great leveller. Being with the same gang for 10 to 14 days in basic conditions, usually in the middle of a field somewhere, helps to break down barriers and defence systems. In these circumstances you begin to hear what their real thoughts and feeling are, because living in this close community causes them to open up.

Over and over again at such camps I have been frustrated that the children of Christian leaders are so often the most unruly, the most messed up, the most cynical and the most disillusioned. Many times I have sat on the grass until way past midnight, wearily trying to get the co-operation of some leader's kid who has come to camp and is causing mayhem. I ask them, "Why do you act this way? What makes you behave this way?" The answers are varied, but the underlying theme in all the answers comes down to the following:

My Dad is a Pastor; he's great in church but you should see how he treats my Mum.

My parents are in leadership and they say good things to other Christians but you should hear them at home.

My parents are in leadership; they have got time for the problems of all the other young people, but they never seem to have time for me.

There are many variations on the theme but you begin to get the picture. Many leader's kids see one thing at home and another thing at church. The result is frustration, confusion and rebellion, but in the middle of the mess is a deep-rooted desire for reality.

Generally in the Church, and I suppose Society at large, it has been assumed that people naturally know how to conduct married life and bring up children. "Well, you just do what comes naturally". I guess that we have been doing that, and some of the results bring tremendous heartache. "Follow the maker's instructions" is the best plan. The Bible does have a lot to say on family life and the upbringing of children.

In the fellowship of which I am part, as I have already said, all prospective married couples go through a pre-marital counselling course, because we *don't* think "it comes naturally". They need helpful instruction from the maker's handbook, the Bible, to get them started and going in the right direction for strong, happy, family life.

Let me share with you some of the things I reckon are basic to bringing up children and dealing with teens in family life.

Openness. We need to be open in our family life; most subjects can and should be aired, including sex, friends, conflicts and family pressures.

Individuality. Children are individuals with opinions, a perspective, likes and dislikes. You can't always follow them, but you can listen to them and try to understand.

Independence. They are going to leave home one day, so you'd better face that fact now. It is helpful therefore to assist to create in their lives self-sufficiency and their own dependence on God, rather than holding on too tightly, and with too many demands. I have noted that parents who tightly hold their children find in teenage years that they become like wet soap. The tighter you squeeze, the easier they jump out of your hand. The children that are held more loosely seem to want to be with their parents when in their teens. To put that in Biblical terms, whatever you hold, you will loose, whatever you let go for the Kingdom's sake, you will find that you have held it and saved it.

Friendship. Most of us hate being "done good to". Yet often that is the approach to children. We need to do them good, but in our doing good to them, they cease to be a person, at least in the way we do them good. Rather they become an object, something that we *react* to rather than *relate* to. I'm sure we need to do things that are good for our children, but we do need to make them our friends. There is a great deal of talk today about friendship and relationship in the Church, and thank God for it, but we need to spread that

88

around in the family quickly. Jesus has made us his friend. I like that, I think that's absolutely fantastic mind-blowing stuff.

Me, a friend of God! He calls me His friend. So why exclude our children, or, dare I say, our wives and husbands? My wife is my best friend and that's how it should be. My children, all three of them, I am proud to have them as my very special friends. Friendship takes the sting out of being a teenager.

Quality Time. We do need to spend time with our families, to strengthen them, but note I said, quality time. Some people spend a lot of time with their families, but I don't think their families notice. Ten minutes of concentrated listening is probably worth 3 hours of reading the newspaper in the house.

Discipline. When it's done with love and started early enough, it's not such a chore. I reckon early enough is before they can talk. If its true that our personalities are set in concrete by the time we are 5 years old, then some of us are just too late. We cannot hope to draw successful lines for teenagers that were not drawn in childhood.

Affirmation. How many times do you hear parents say negative things about their children, such as, "I can't do anything with them"? With that negative expression you never will. Don't tell people your child is hopeless or a failure, and certainly do not tell the child that. Make them know they are loved, appreciated, wanted, respected, not with false praise, but real genuine congratulations when it is warranted. To reiterate Dr. Donald Howard's statement, "Most children do more things right than they do wrong, but we spend far more time correcting the wrong things than we do strengthening that which is already right".

Chapter 21

Conflict

Conflict is part of life. We are never going to avoid it.
Good, right, loving, friendship-related confrontation,
that may result in conflict, is healthy for all of us.

It does seem to me that some people live in
permanent conflict. I don't know how they survive
the pressure. Perhaps they don't or won't survive.
There are others at the opposite end of the scale who
never confront and never attempt to. They live with
so many unresolved conflicts that I wonder how they
survive or sustain any lasting relationships. Perhaps
they don't. Then there is the other group of people
who are so volatile that they confront at the drop of
a hat. I call them "land mine" people. You tread on
the spot and they explode.

I heard Terry Virgo say a very useful comment
about confrontation. "Of course it needs to be done,
but it's a bit like an operation. There's a need for
preparation by both surgeon and patient and the
conditions need to be the best possible, with the

patient being carefully prepared for surgery." He went on to say that some people tackled confrontation like surgery, except that if amputation was necessary, they would approach it with so little preparation and the minimum of compassion, resulting in the limb being lopped off in the corridor and the patient being left to bleed to death.

We need to confront, but Ecclesiastes says that there is a season or time for everything under heaven. When you confront, choose the time, prepare the patient and bind up the wounds afterwards.

Many parents, particularly during the onset of teenage years, turn into nags. During this time young people experiment, test the limits, put pressure on what we call norms, and check the real values. Not all of this is bad. Some of the things that we disagree with were just our norms, neither right nor wrong, neither moral nor immoral, just our way of doing it, and there may be another way and perhaps our teenager has just found it.

I'm sure there will be correction needed at times and discipline/confrontation too, but might I make a plea for sanity here. If you tackle every issue you disagree with or have another view on or a difference of opinion on, you will become that terrible nag-bag that all teenagers hate. You'll never stop, and alienation will set in. You will not attract, train and release, quite the reverse; you will set a virtually indestructable wall between you and your teen. It's far better to choose the field of conflict and tackle only major issues, and choose the time and place. If possible, take the high ground, be rational, listen well, don't bawl, and never, even if all else fails, say, "Because I say so!". It's usually a very weak unprocessed argument, although I have to confess that I have used it on occasions.

You will discover that if you are wise in your choice of confrontational issues and handle people with respect, then you will win friendship. You will know when you are getting through when you are voluntarily consulted and your opinions sought after by your own teenager.

It can be done and you can do it!

Chapter 22

Training Children

I have often thought, "Why isn't there a better name for children than children?" "Small Adult" seems better to me. In some way this chapter will summarise much of what has been said about attracting, training and releasing youth. The earlier we start with our youth, the ones we've got, – our own children, – then the better it is.

Growth brings a continued level of understanding, knowledge, maturity, and for those who know God, wisdom. Yet we often seem to ignore what is already there, on the way up. I've often heard parents say, "Well, you can't slap or discipline a baby, can you? It doesn't understand." This "doesn't understand" stance then progresses right through to teenage years. I reckon babies know far more than we give credit for, and are quite capable of knowingly manipulating Mum and Dad even before they can speak. One can see things learned before speech then used by the toddler when they can speak, even when the child is seven or eight: Things such as the tantrum fit for example, I've seen seven year olds throw themselves on the floor, foot-stamping by the later age group, pouting, very noisily crying, even clinging to a parent to stay at home or take them out, all learned and usually well operative before the child is two years old. Personally, I believe firm, loving, discipline starts at birth. Right from that early stage our sinful nature begins to urgently exercise its will, and that desire for its own way emerges more and more, day by day.

Notwithstanding the discipline side of growing up, children, I believe, need to be listened to, consulted, and even learned from. There is often an understanding that a child will clearly have, that an adult needs to re-learn. In group situations children are often more sensitive to wrong atmospheres, wrong pressures, wrong manipulation, and often frighteningly honest in their assessments and judgements, often expressing clearly what was under the surface, but had failed to be acknowledged by the adult. I don't, however, think we should then allow the child to always express those opinions or to be rude and precocious. They do need to learn the social graces of the culture in which they live and how to get along with others.

"Spoilt" is a word we often use. What do I mean by that? A spoilt child is one who through parental action has unconsciously been led to believe that the world revolves around him or her. Dad and Mum pander to every request. They are placed at the centre of attraction on every occasion. Bad habits and wrong behaviour are excused by, "Well, that's how they are," or "Aren't they funny?" or "Now dear," giving them the impression early on that in fact they were made to be pampered. Of course they are not, no child is. This type of upbringing, where the child is in control, is extremely cruel. Throughout life they won't be controlled, at school, in the office, at the work place.

Unfortunately what happens is that the growing child does not understand what is wrong. They haven't been taught to be giving, not always the centre of attraction, considerate of others, and so their actions repel people. They have a lack of friends.

Teachers have a problem with them. As they grow up, even when they move into the adult world their demanding ways make them a pain in the neck. Their opinion, actions, desires, perspective, is always seen as the right one. People tolerate them, find it hard to befriend them, and take enormous risks at confrontation. Some understand and say, "Poor thing, they were spoilt," behind their back, but it doesn't help the individual. A spoilt, pampered childhood can lead to a deficient life in every way. It is a most unkind act.

It will not do to say, "I can't discipline them; he won't do anything I say; I can't control her; I'm unable to be firm." Steel yourself, love the child and discipline. Remember, an undisciplined child is an unloved child. They have never been really loved.

Others take the easy option. When told to clean their room and the child doesn't, Mum, with some grumbling, does. This is a cop out. Of course, in one sense, it is easier to clean it than to persevere in the discipline of making the child do it. But in the long term it is much harder; you will always be cleaning the room. You aren't being kind, you are being unkind, spoiling the child, making him or her incomplete in that area.

But, don't over-discipline. Always explain why, and if not understood, explain again. Be friends. Handled right even a very young child can be an excellent friend, and very good company. There were many times when I have been with adults for an evening and their foolish approach to life has made me wish I had spent the evening with my young children, as their company was far better.

How about some do's and don'ts for bringing up children?

(My version of course:-)

Do be an example.

Don't say one thing yourself and do another.

Do encourage.

Don't compare with others.

Do discipline.

Don't break their spirit (Overdiscipline).

Do be friends.

Don't spoil.

Do explain.

Don't say, "Because I say so."

Do ensure tasks are fair and completed.

Don't allow a child to avoid a responsibility.

Do discipline firmly for rebellion.

Don't discipline for genuine mistakes.

Do set lines that should not be crossed.

Don't allow children to dictate everything.

Do love one another in the family, especially Mother and Father.

Don't put the child at the centre.

Do give tasks and responsibilities.

Don't grumble and do the tasks for them.

Do support Mum or Dad's discipline in front of the children.

Don't take parental sides against one another and on the side of the child.

Do produce Godly men and women.

Don't miss it!

Chapter 23

Children and Teen Prayer

One of the most powerful things I ever saw was one Sunday morning, when I preached on the important place that children have in the church, and that we must not wait until they are old for them to win people to Christ, pray for the sick, get baptised in water and the Holy Spirit, and generally learn to minister to one another. After preaching about these things I asked people who needed prayer to come forward. I then asked for children under the age of 11 years old who were filled with the Holy Spirit to go and pray for those who had come forward. It was dynamite as the youngsters laid hands on these towering adults and ministered in power with words of knowledge and wisdom, unassuming but expectant. God, after all, is their God, and we are commanded to enter the Kingdom with the kind of trust that children have. I saw afresh on that occasion how much in church life we rob the children from fully participating in the Body.

Children's prayers are simple and faith-filled.

I have noticed in our three Christian schools how easily, when set the right example, children and young teens take to prayer, especially when it's not formalised. We arranged voluntary midday prayer meetings for the students that were well attended. Their prayers were simple and faith filled. Having been taught that God is a loving Heavenly Father, who will respond to their best interests, they prayed in faith believing.

I have seen members of staff who have been ready to go home because of sickness, being challenged by a student and asked, "has anyone yet prayed for you?" On being told "No", they then asked, "May I pray for you?" Having done just that, I have seen the member of staff back at work within ten minutes.

I am impressed that when challenged many of our teens will turn up to pray all night. I believe that we rob children by sending them out of our prayer and worship to play, or encouraging them to draw during the meeting of the Body of Christ for worship and ministry. I believe that if your services are lively enough, powerful enough, active enough, with the manifest presence of God, then children and young teens will not want to play and draw, rather they will delight to become active participants in what God is doing.

Ishmael is invited to take charge of many of the largest childrens/family events in the U.K. I know that he has placed a strong emphasis on children not just being ministered to but actively ministering to the Body. I have heard him relate on many occasions the blessing of children's and teen's answered prayer, words of knowledge, gifts of healing etc. Why exclude this valuable part of the Body?

When I was a child I hated some of the things that were done in church life. I hated being sent out to the children's class. I hated children's church and songs. I hated being excluded from the main Body of Christ. I earnestly wanted to play my part. I wasn't even counted when they checked how many were present. What a shame! I think it should change and I reckon many children and teens would agree.

Chapter 24

Christian Education

When talking about this subject, one has to climb over people's prejudices, preconceptions, muddled thinking and emotional rather than rational hostility, particularly when talking with Christians and Christian leaders. At the risk of being repetitive, I have to say, I have seen it work.

In meetings and committees, where I have the opportunity to say how Christian education works, I have been met with a total blank wall by people who are there to ask how can we attract train and release young people. Many times these same people would share their failures, but my answers were still unacceptable.

I can see that it may not be the total answer, hence the many chapters to this book – but I still believe it's part of the answer. If it wasn't so sad it would be amusing to hear leaders who have young people who are in a mess, their own children included, unable to listen to an answer because of prejudice and an inability to break out of conditioned thinking, so much so that they are even unwilling to hear that Christian Education might be an answer. I do not say this from a position of failure, but from a position of "Hey! this is working for me. Would you like to share in some of the benefits and blessings of what's going on?"

Let me give you a concrete example of what I mean. A member of one such committee was sharing how, as a leader in his church, he found he could not motivate his young people. He also said that after a certain age, roughly 14/15 years, his church would lose young people. He then went on to say that his own children were in a total mess and could we pray for them? I joined the discussion by saying I have found that Christian Education is an answer in some of these areas of church and family life. The man in question responded quickly, "Oh, that's ridiculous; that is no answer; we don't want hot-house plants", in other words "I don't want my children in a controlled environment". Even the chairman of the committee verbally jumped on me saying, "You must not impose your views on us. Just because you think it's the answer, it doesn't mean that it is".

I do not pretend to know all the dynamics of Christian Education, but let me simply deal with some of the positive things that I say in relationship to the subject of this book. I'm sure that leaders of churches, fathers and mothers, people of Christian belief and persuasion want to attract, train and release their teenagers in a positive way.

Christian Education is a positive step in this direction.

I have seen in church life how a Christian school affects young people's thinking, where church is positive, and church is a place of knowledge and wisdom. Providing the school is central to a live church, church is fun; church is a place of friendship; church is a place of spirit. Church is where I meet God and find Him to be a friend. Church is where I find good heroes.

It goes on from there and I have observed as some of our young people have gone out into the big wide world to college, university, secular jobs, that they have become thankful for their Christian Education. They see that we have given them a balanced world view; we have taught them to study well. They have learned to think for themselves and are firm in their beliefs, not swayed by work mates. So much for the usual "hot house" comments that suggest that people won't cope when they go out to work.

In our own situation we have found that Christian Education has an effect on the thinking of the whole church, and so young people who don't go to our schools nevertheless are inspired and motivated by the ethos of the School. I don't pretend to understand it all completely, but I do see it happening and I like what I see, that is, well-balanced young people who are coping with the pressures of life and generally enjoying life, young people in the church who are keen to go on with God, and have a desire to do great things for God, people with what I call "Holy ambition", not

106

drifters, not disillusioned with God or church, but the opposite.

What do you want? An answer to the problem which often vexes church leaders, or do you prefer to stay with your fears and your problems? In the end, I guess it's up to you.

Chapter 25

Having Spiritual Children

We live in the age of Bible Colleges, with an away-course-mentality. We recognise that training is essential in almost all areas of life, but we are conditioned in the West to thinking that training entails going away, or sending people to special institutions.

We find that was not the way Jesus did it. He lived with His trainees for three years, travelled with them, slept with them, talked much with them, worked with them and, if they had such things in those days, probably went on holiday with them. People's comments give a lot away. They didn't note where they had been trained. What they said was, "you can tell these people have been with Jesus". Why so? Well it's obvious really. You get like the people you are with; somehow you imbibe what they are.

I reckon its time for the Church, and particularly the leaders in our churches to begin to have spiritual children. Now it may hurt to say so, but you don't have spiritual children by running Bible studies, beginners courses, family training programmes, seminars or any other in-house or away-day teaching programme. Recently I was on a working party where the subject of spiritual children came up. A leader of a large church said "Yes, that's what we need, and I have planned a series of Sunday morning services to teach it". I reckon he missed it.

In reality, the way to teach successfully is the way Jesus did. He took time, living, eating, communicating, under the same roof. In other words it's the imparting of your life. You will then pass on who and what you are, and that's okay if you are following Jesus closely.

I can hear some say, "Well that way of teaching was alright for Bible days, but this is nearly the 21st Century". Well it might be, but people are still people.

I've tried Bible College, I've tried sermons, and house parties, and special Sunday morning speakers, and all those have their place, but the people I've taught the best have lived with me, to a greater or lesser degree.

It's hard though, having someone else's kids living with you. I've done it four or five times so far; not just for a couple of days, but months, even years on end. That can be a lot of pressure; an extra mouth to feed, extra teenage hassle, extra pressure on space. It costs, that's why some of you won't do it, even if it's not a question of living with you, but the adopting of youngsters who you will take with you when you go to a conference, to minister in another town or fellowship, or take along when you are overseas. It's all extra pressure, time, effort, and cost, and some of us would rather not get involved, but if we don't it won't produce the goods.

I'm sorry to have to point out that this type of teaching is costly, but you get what you pay for. What do you want? A youth group or spiritual children? If we were in discussion, and you listed to me all the reasons why you don't have people live with you in your home in middle class suburbia, or why you don't take a youngster with you here, there and everywhere, I would have to say it's a cop out. You don't want spiritual children.

I *do* want spiritual children, and I can assure you they are great and worth the cost.

"Do not store up for yourselves treasures on earth where moth. . . ."

Chapter 26

Non-materialistic Goals

Most people in the West somehow manage to afford what they want to afford. It is easy to pay lip service to the fact that we ought to lay up treasures in Heaven where neither moth nor rust corrupts. In practice we want tangible things now and we demonstrate this in a thousand different ways.

For a while I moved around the U.K. talking with church groups of all denominations about Christian education. If you asked parents a positive question like, "Do you want your children to go on with God?", you would get a straight answer, "Yes – of course." However if you posed the question, "if your children couldn't take State exams, had no hope of a career, were unable to get qualifications, yet they were assured of going on with God, which one would you choose?" For most there would be great consternation. No direct answer would be forth-coming, people would bluster, be embarassed, ask questions but avoid giving straight answers. Usually if you got an answer it would be, "Well, they need to get on."

I may have a jaundiced view, but after much travelling I came to the conclusion that in most of the places I visited if it was straight choice of knowing God or going to university, university would win every time. And this was from church-going parents who believed the Bible, or said they did! They went to church regularly, took the children to Sunday School but underneath was a strong materialism that directed the whole of life.

Over the past ten years we have become so concerned with owning our own house it has almost become the be-all and end-all of life.

It is no good telling friends and children that the home in Heaven is the most important and believe in extending the Kingdom, when in reality extending the patio takes a far higher priority than everything else. The action is what will be communicated at the end of the day. When people are relaxed they tend to talk about what really matters to them. What do you talk about – the house, the car, the job, the latest requirement, sport? It's not wrong to talk about any of these things, but I do believe we can notice the topic that arises in our minds most of the time – it's usually our priority, and sadly it is often materialistic, not Kingdom. That's where we are and will communicate through whatever words we use.

It's not wrong to have a nice car, live in a decent house and not have to scrape for every penny. But how do we hold them? Often we will know when God puts His finger on it. "*Abraham, give me your* son". So God catches and checks us, sets right our priorities, but have we then left the teens we have influenced trapped with decaying materialistic goals?

What we need, to quote one of the elder's wives in North London is to, "Always hold these things with loose hands." That will communicate.

Chapter 27

Clichés

Clichés are almost always wrong. I reckon the golden rule about every cliché is to question it. Usually they are setting wrong mind sets, wrong models, wrong methods and even if they are a correct statement of fact, then the fact needs to be challenged. Our thinking needs to be changed. I am also suspicious about scripture verses that are quoted in cliché form. I usually find that they are out of context, only half a statement or completely wrong.

Here are some of my pet hates:

1. "All teenagers go through a rebellious stage."

No they don't. I know lots of teenagers that didn't and didn't want to either. They admittedly often come from well-adjusted families, and had strong Christian influence, though not always.

2. "Leaders' kids only see the negatives."

Well if your leaders' kids only see the negatives then more fool you, and what a problem and joyless service for the King you must have had. My children certainly see negatives, but I would say the privileges of being in a leader's home, knowing what was afoot in the Kingdom was far more exciting and outweighed any of the negatives.

3. "Ministers' kids are always more of a problem."

No they're not. Mine weren't for a start. In fact they were almost always an asset to the work, often making things possible to do that could never have been done without them and I know other kids who are just the same.

4. "The children must come first."

No they shouldn't. Especially in the home. Parents should love one another. Naturally they should put God first, and the children third. That will give them stability and security.

5. "What are young people coming to?"

Well it may be good, it may be bad, but probably we had something to do with it influence-wise, and if it's bad we had better keep quiet.

6. "When I was young it was so different."

It probably was, but probably not as good or as glamorous as our bad memory now thinks it was.

7. "If you had lived as long as me then you wouldn't say that."

Well, people said just that sort of thing for years and I find the opposite is usually true. Some of what I said when I was younger was right and I'm even more convinced in that opinion now.

8. "Youngsters have it easy these days."

Well, I'm sure they do in some areas. However have you ever thought of the inward pressures that are put on them, vice, T.V., heavy advertising etc?

9. "Don't do as I do, do as I say."

This attitude leads to rebellion, hypocrisy and a loss of your teenager, when referring to T.V or something else that is a bad influence.

10. "Oh, it won't hurt, they don't understand."

Of course they do, and what you are doing in putting that thought into their minds is wrong. The Bible tells us that what goes into our minds will affect us. That's why God effects change in us by renewing our mind.

Clichés. Check them. They are a direction to a mind-set that probably ·needs changing.

Chapter 28

Freedom

Freedom must be the most talked about word of the 90's, but what is freedom? It is obvious from the Bible and from history that people find what they call freedom, strange, not what they had expected, sometimes unwelcome. Often what they call freedom is not freedom at all, rather it is a step to a new kind of master or hedonism.

It's obvious the children of Israel were not pleased when, in the midst of their slavery, God's man, Moses, came to lead them to freedom. They were interested in slightly improving their lot under the domination of Pharaoh. In fact if you had really pressed the Israelites as to what they wanted, they would have probably replied, "we like eating cucumbers in our diet, we'd like more garlic and couldn't Pharaoh please do something about the market price of onions?" They saw Moses as a troublemaker, a disturber of the status quo and of course he was. Pray God keeps such people coming.

I've always reckoned that one of the reasons Peter walked free from prison, putting on his shoes, going past the Roman guards through the various doors, was only because he thought he was dreaming. If he hadn't thought so he probably would have found that freedom was impossible. And as for the great men of faith praying for his release, just like us, I reckon they were making lots of noise, probably walking round the room, naming it and claiming it, making great verbal statements of belief, yet when Peter knocked on the door, the expectancy of his release was zero. God is so gracious, isn't he?

If we are bound, if we are enslaved, if we are in bondage, then we need to be set free. But being set free is often a more painful process than we expected it to be. I hope it won't be painful for Eastern Europe, but some of the birth pains of new freedom are still strong, as we are seeing right at the beginning.

Yet, God's plan is for us to be free. Often He will force the pace. In our church it's often the young who are flexible enough to see that what we have made so sacrosanct is not worth a fig to God, and He is going to disturb our stultifying bondage and set us free. Wonderful freedom. Well, for some perhaps but for others it's not so wonderful. The freedom to clap was greeted with, "We don't need that terrible noise in our church." The freedom to extend musical instruments from organ and piano to a whole cacophony of glorious praise was greeted with, "Well, it's alright for the youth." And lots of churches still have not got there.

Dancing is still greeted in many areas with a very

"Don't be silly Rhoda! I know we are praying for him, but he is hardly likely to turn up *yet!*"

disapproving eye, as if to say there is no knowing where this will lead to. Perhaps to the Red Sea, eh?

One could go on, but I think the point is made. God wants us free, free to fly, and I think He will sometimes set us free against our own balanced, sensible judgement. He will set us free even if at the beginning it causes us pain. Anyway, in the end it's great. And wouldn't you know it, He will often use that God-appointed, non voted in, non-committee, goodness-knows-where-he-came-from, God-anointed youngster to do it.

Chapter 29

College Students

College students are part of the youth scene and it's as important to attract, train and release these people as it is anyone else. Churches seem to have funny ideas about students. I've talked with church leaders in the past who say things like, "Oh, I don't get too involved with students, here today, gone tomorrow." Others have said to me, "Yes, we love students but we don't involve them too much in the life of the church as you won't keep them." A third view I've come across is perhaps marginally better. It seems to be the view that, "These students need to be done-good-unto and as we are a college town/university city we must put on special things for students so that we can be seen to be ministering to them."

One problem with the third approach is that it tends to see people as students, *what* they are, rather than *who* they are, people first. Studying is what they are doing. We see them as fodder for the ministry of our church, "souls to be saved", rather than the people

whom Christ died for and who we need to get to know for our sake and theirs.

When I was in the north of England struggling in a tiny congregation, some of the first people that started to swell the size of the fellowship numerically were students. I was desperately in need of people. I didn't know the attitudes above, I just saw them as people we needed to strengthen the church by their gifts. We involved them; they became Sunday school teachers and youth leaders, in fact they were totally integrated into the life of the church. Some of them moved permanently to the area. They would stay in the church rather than go home for the long holiday in the summer. In short they became committed members. My experience in London has not been very different. I believe there is a right approach with students.

1. When they first come, give them a chance to see the area. We used to talk with students, give them a welcome, and invite them for a meal but with no strings attached. We would encourage them to have a look at at the church life generally in the area.

2. After a short period of time we would say, "we want you, but if this is not to be your spiritual home, your local church, then find somewhere that is, but don't attend six different churches." If allowed to develop that can be a fatal student sickness from which many never seem to recover. They never become committed anywhere and therefore useless to a local church situation.

3. We would seek quickly to integrate the person

and find God's gifts through them for the benefit of the church.

We discovered that many were involved in the college Christian Union and the church often became involved too. Nevertheless we became their local church, their spiritual home and their friends. They eventually bought their houses in our area, married and stayed in our area. They became the leaders of the church. We had got, trained and, for many, released them into wider ministries.

Students are just people at college!

Chapter 30

Great Expectations

I want to see the purpose of God in my generation. I want to see the purpose of God while I am alive. But I can't do that alone. God never intended me to. I am part of a Body, part of an army, a team, so I have to play my part with others. I am required by the King to build others up; they are required to provoke and encourage me.

It is true that as we give and take responsibilities, as we seek to stretch one another in the work of God, there will be mistakes. Some will not quite make the grade we expected them to at this time. There will probably be another time. Yet, what we have got is what we have got. What we are is what we are and where we are is where we are. So start! Whatever we have we can use to begin. Take steps, set goals, put down time limits and assess progress.

I am not disappointed with today's young people. I am not disillusioned by them. I am confident that they are seeking to be God's men and women. I am sure that God is using them and will use them more. I believe they, in the hands of the Father, saved by the Son, equipped by the Holy Spirit, can do it. They can do more than me, more than you, and they need to. They, along with you and I, can be the ones that bring in the Kingdom. My expectations for attracting, training and releasing are high. Couldn't yours be too?